The Power
of
Serving Others

By:

Stephen Gill

With A Special Foreword by

Michelle Crowell

Foreword:

It is an honor and privilege to have been asked to write this forward for my precious brother. I had my first encounter with Stephen Gill (Be Real Steve) back in summer of 2019. I had just joined the Rescue Me Project and we were both mutual speakers at the local juvenile detention center in our area. To know Steve is to love him. His very presence demands attention and a listening ear. His ability to get across his message in a way that is easily understood is amazing. Every audience is captivated by his ability to poetically flow with such ease.

I have been blessed over the last 2 years to serve with Steve in many instances. Whether speaking to middle and high schoolers on identity, ministering to those who are in drug recovery facilities, juvenile detention centers, or just to other church congregations, I can honestly say that Steve has a true heart for others and exhibits his heart through servanthood.

As a fellow published author and speaker, I was excited to hear that Steve was finally writing his first book. When I first heard about his book, "The Power of Serving," I was intrigued. I thought to myself, who does not realize how great it is to serve others. What I did not consider was that many people do not realize the true benefit of serving others. As one who also has a servant's heart, I find myself at times frustrated by those who are all takers and no givers.

This book will cause you to take a step back and think about what you are doing to serve your fellow man. You will take a journey with Steve throughout his life and the many opportunities he has encountered to offer his service, how to genuinely love others without condition. I found myself smiling at times while crying at others.

We are all called to love and serve one another. I like to say that we are truly the hands and feet of Jesus. I am honored to call Steve my friend, my brother in Christ. I believe this book will touch your heart just as it did mine and bless your soul as you seek out ways you may serve your fellow man. Be blessed.

Michelle Crowell

Introduction

Much thought and consideration went into the spiritual birth of this book. I had a broad visual image in my mind, but I lacked motivation and experience. It was as if God was telling me that I needed to see more within life before concluding this manuscript. On one beautiful August afternoon, I found myself in the center of The Bridge-street Mall, a spacious outdoor shopping center in Huntsville, Alabama. It was clouded on this given Sunday after church, and I needed the small escape. The temperature was just right for a nice read on a bench. The smiles on the faces of shoppers were endless. I saw couples holding hands, pushing strollers, and shopping until they dropped. Something inside of me gave the impression that most of these persons were truly happy in life. Just the sight of these things lifted my heart and spirit. Before I knew it, I felt my cheek muscles rising into position and yes, I too found myself smiling. However, that is not what moved me the most. It was this young man who had drawn such a crowd in the mall's square. He was simply playing instrumentals on a small speaker while he blew his soul through the bronze neck of his worn-out saxophone. Whites, Mexicans, Latinos and African Americans were there in an awe of amazement while this young man simply used his God given ability to serve people. An elderly woman sitting next to me even got up and slow danced with her husband of 42 years while listening to the rhythm and flow of this individual. No one opposed his presence. Without even knowing it, they embraced it with a sense of ease and excitement. Visitors from near and far applauded, danced, cried, and even dropped big bucks in his little tin can. This young man did much more than inspire a few people; he served them in ways unimaginable. In ways that he would probably never know. I had just witnessed the "Power of Serving Others", which thus gave way to the birth of this book you are now reading. Enjoy!

"Born to Serve"

Way before the marijuana, liquor, and wild southern nights, I can honestly say that I learned to serve God at a young age. I grew up at 1226 Aloe street in Cleveland, Mississippi, in the heart of the Delta, where dope boys ran the streets and preachers filled the weekly revivals. That majestic address is tattooed within the living room of my heart. It is where I was blessed, and it is also where I was cursed. However, throughout the latter parts of this book, you will get a clearer understanding of what I desire to convey to you with that statement.

My family and I have never been strangers to religion, nor to those soul filled Baptist churches that were planted on almost every street corner in town. There's one church that stands out, and it was called Old Saint Phillip Missionary Baptist Church, our family church. Imprinted on the cornerstone was my grandfather's name, who helped build it in the early 1900's. Every Sunday morning, my Mother or Grandmother would get me, my brothers and cousins dressed for that sacred meeting at what we called the "Church House". Old folks back then did not allow us to do any and everything in the Church House. I was blessed to come up in a time where the elderly women wore the big ole hats on their heads and white gloves on their hands. Those old ushers would take a child in the back of the church and wear them out if they got out of hand in the sanctuary.

Because of that, I still have the utmost respect for that special room where God's Holy Word goes forth. In later years, I grew to find out that some churches referred to the sanctuary as an auditorium. I could never get use to calling God's room an auditorium while knowing the history from which I was raised. Back then, when your parents or grandparents whipped you, there was no such thing as calling Human Services or telling your schoolteachers. As a matter of fact, the teachers themselves were able to put the belt to your back side. There was one whipping, I mean beating, that we received from our

Grandmother that I will never forget. One Sunday, she gave us all 25 cents to put in church. Most times, Grandma would stay at home on Sundays when her health gave her too many problems. However, with that quarter in hand, we came up with a most clever idea. We decided to travel to the candy lady's house across the street from the church and spend our offering money on penny candy. Up to now, I cannot tell you who told Grandma about our mischievous act, but that beating will forever be stitched within my soul.

"Born to Serve!!"

I cannot speak for everyone, but when God

gives me the opportunity to serve someone,

the moment feels just right, as if I was born to

serve. I will never forget how good it felt on

that warm Saturday afternoon of the year

1998. At the time, I was 10yrs old. I did not

have a single goal for life in mind. I was simply

free. In those days, bike riding was popular.

We would ride for hours just sightseeing,

racing, popping a wheelie, or traveling to see

a group of girls. Wherever we went, bike

riding was our main form of getting there.

Well on this day while cruising down a road

called Old Highway 61, we discovered this

elderly white lady mowing her yard in the heat

of the day. It had to be well beyond 90

degrees outside and from the look of her

stature, she appeared to be in her late eighties. Before I knew it, I had jumped off 20" Chrome object with wheels, so that I could make myself available for some type of service to someone in need. "Ma'am, do you need any help?" "I sure do she replied!!!" It felt so great to push that Old Ancient looking lawn mower across her gigantic front lawn. She pointed her fingers in the direction of paper and weeds, but we did not mind because it felt so right. After we were done, a hot meal was cooked, and laughter took place within the center of that old sweet lady's kitchen. We never did learn her name, but in the months to come we no longer saw her extremely long Chevrolet car parked in the yard. We only saw 3-foot grass now surrounding her house like a military Police Swat Unit. I thought maybe she had passed on from this life to be with the Lord, but whenever I pass by, that gracious memory of serving her still warms my heart.

Born to Serve!

I once heard an elderly man say that, "it is not the lack of ability that holds most people back, it is the lack of opportunity!!!" That statement has come to be one of my all-time favorites and it continues to burst with a great deal of significance. It reigns true in New York, the Middle East, Chicago, as well as Mississippi.

If young people are not given the opportunity at a young age, then their fire for serving others may never be ignited.

Proverbs 22:6 tell us to train up a child in the way he or she should go. When I was a kid, I had a best friend named Moon. I know that is an uncommon name for a child, but he was my best friend and whenever you saw me, you saw him. Moon was raised in an apartment with his mom and sickly grandfather. Once I learned more, I realized that Moon's mother was raised by her dad and she tried her best to serve him in his old age. However, this task grew to be extremely hard and almost impossible because of her sickness. There would be times when Moon and I would be riding our bicycles and we would see his mom staggering out of a rundown crack houses. It was no secret; it was public business on what my poor little friend had to go through within the walls of that one room apartment. Kids would say," That's why your mom is a crackhead!!!" Instantly, you would see anger overshadow his presence while he would tighten his fists. At times, my mom would allow him to stay the night, and periodically, take him to church with us. Most times, at the dinner tables, by looking at him, he seemed to be a fish out of water. It was like, he desired to love like us, give like us, and serve like us but his upbringing stripped him of that blessed opportunity. In fact, there would be moments where he tried to bring another side of himself out but when the world opened her curtains, he would calmly shut down on stage of life. I thought about him a great deal after I moved off to Georgia in 2007, only to find out that Moon was actually SERVING- not people but time in prison. I then realized that every child needs positive people to help us on this stage called life. I'm not making excuses, but if my friend's family had someone to serve and help them early on, I believe his fate would have been much different.

"You win some, you lose some."

I know we all would like to believe that we will

help save everyone we encounter. Well my

brothers and sisters, that is just not the case.

Chances are, at some point your heart will get

shattered and you will spend countless nights

praying for those who just do not seem to get

it. Sometimes we do not truly realize the hurt

and pain that has been inflicted upon most of

the individuals that we come in contact with.

I'm reminded of a young man that I had the

pleasure of mentoring for a little over a year.

His name was Drew, a 15-year-old kid who

simply needed a true brother figure in his life.

After leaving a restaurant one night,

something strange happened. Drew had this

presence about himself that caused me to question what was going on in his heart. He began telling me about the years of hurt that he faced with his family being so distant and his father not being around. Tears started to roll down his face and his cry for help was evident. His story was so heart wrenching. It was as if the moon itself had to hide behind the prodigious clouds so that we could not see it weep the night away. Drew even opened about his mom being married but not truly focusing on her marriage nor her children like she should have. He felt so abandoned and helpless from the hand that his life had dealt him. I instantly asked myself, "*What can I do to help*!!!"

Then, the Lord placed the answer so clearly within my spirit: I can serve. I can encourage. I can try my best to allow God's glorious light to shine through me. So, I did exactly that. Each week I made it my aim to spend as much time with Drew as possible. He accompanied me on my motivational speaking engagements and to all my weekly bible studies. As time went on, there was a significant change in Drew's heart and life. The transformation was not immediate or easily accomplished but he fought, he pressed on, and he maintained a sense of persistence.

Before I knew it, the rain clouds of shame had moved out of the way, thus giving way to a blessed ray of hope. I no longer had to ask

him to get ready for church. He would call

asking me what was the hold up, especially if I

did not show up right on time. It still makes

me smile to even think back on those

transitioning days. While Drew was still within

his Cocoon stage of growth, I myself found a

certain change coming over me. I didn't

realize that in the process of serving others,

we discover a newness about ourselves that

we never knew was there. That is why I

believed God places each of us here, to find

eternal purpose in the lives we change but

also the lives that help change us.

While driving from church one night, Drew

mentioned to me that he was no longer selling

drugs and that he had no desire to smoke it.

Words cannot describe how great I felt at that

very moment. It was like a Father seeing his

only child walk the stage at graduation night

after struggling for many years with his

academics. Not many days after this grand

announcement, I received a letter that I was

accepted into a Bible University in Alabama.

Drew was heartbroken to find out that I would

be leaving Mississippi, knowing that for the

past year of his life, I was the only true brother

he had. I assured him that I would make

periodic visits and that I would always be a

phone call away if he ever needed spiritual

advice. He accepted my plea with open arms,

and he came to grips with my sad departure.

Life on college the college campus was extremely life changing for me. It did not take long to realize that the school was predominantly white and that it truly did not have a broad enrollment of Christian believers of the African American descent. So, at times I had to smile when nothing was funny and scratch when nothing on my body itched. It is extremely hard for an individual when you do not have friends nor family in your new land. In order to find peace from the tedious class load and the twenty pages reports, I made it my custom to drive 25 minutes west of the school where I could get a grand sight of the Tennessee River. It was located right off the Natchez trace. This is where I engaged in the best meditation. In fact, If I got a chance to arrive before the sun went down, I got a chance to see God color the sky. On this warm Saturday evening, I had no idea that it would turn out to be one of the saddest days of my life. After spending hours at the River, I returned to my car, only to discover five missed calls and numerous text messages. One message I will never forget. It was from a high school friend. For the sake of confidentiality, I'll call him Ronny. He sent a message asking me, "Have you heard the news about Drew!!!" My heart dropped and my intuition prompt me that it was not a moment of celebration but that of sadness. Later I discovered that Drew was gunned down by a rival gang on the vicious streets of Mississippi. Instantly my mind started racing so I turned to the holy scriptures for answers. Lord, what did I do wrong as a mentor? Why was it impossible for my words to save him? What came over him to cause him to get back connected with negative associates? After days of grappling with a variety of questions, the answer pierced my spirit like a two-edged sword. It was simply this, "You will win some and lose some but you cannot save them all!" We must never forget that God used prison as a waiting place for Joseph because his story would be vital to others one day. He also can use the death of some to bring about life to others.

In 2016, I stated working at a Youth Juvenile Detention Center as a counselor and for half a year, I was the Unit Director. Now that I look back over my life, I realize that working there was totally apart of God's majestic plan. Before getting hired, a friend and I got the grand opportunity of speaking to the kids there in 2015. While there, we observed the lack of love shown to the teens from the faculty and staff. It was like they were simply there to collect a paycheck and not truly cater to the brokenness of those precious teens. We made our way to the car afterwards and said a simple prayer. "Lord, send some counselors here that truly love you and those who care for your children!"

A year later I was sitting in an orientation class of a local car dealership in Florence Alabama. For the first time in my life, I was about to attempt the field as a car salesman. But once I found out that I had to lie here and there, my interest began to dwindle. While taking an exam on a how a salesman should approach a customer, I was urged by the Holy Spirit to go to indeed.com. Well, I did and the first job I saw was the detention center that my friend and I spoke at the previous year. I instantly knew exactly what God was doing. That prayer of sending God-fearing counselors to that facility was answered. I was the man God was waiting on. I was instantly hired, and God moved me from counselor to supervisor to Unit Director in the span of a year. I now sit back and smile at the mighty hand of God. As Unit Director, I had the authority to hire whomever I chose with the approval from the Program Director. That career was the best job I have ever served in outside of preaching. My heart was touched deeply by the young men I have met along that journey. To this very day, I still receive success phone calls from some of them who have graduated from the program and gone to college. In my book, that's a win. You win some and you lose some, but the good fight of faith continues!

Contrary to popular belief, serving others comes with its ups and downs. This chapter will discuss how serious serving others is and how this world cannot exist without these determined few. There are many things in history that moves me but nothing fascinates me more than the immense power found in the soul of the Civil Rights Movement. Never in American history have we read of such a movement. I mean, people from all different walks of life found a common interest based on love and the desire to serve others. This force somehow convicted the conscience of the world like nothing else could. Many like Dr. Martin Luther King, Fannie Lou Hamer, and Nelson Mandela went down in history as some of the world's greatest servants.

However, we often push these mighty men

and women of valor to the forefront, only to

forget the bravest soldiers who never had a

crowd of fans to remember their names. In

fact, most of these forgotten heroes and

sheros names went unheard within the ears of

many who have studied history. One powerful

activist comes to mind when this topic arises.

Her name is Constance Curry, a Caucasian

field representative of the American Friends

Service Committee (AFSC).

Mrs. Curry fought long and hard to make it

possible for the Carter's, an all-black family of

Drew, Mississippi, to gain their rightful place in

the land of the free. She would periodically

drive to a plantation in Mississippi to interview

Mae Bertha Carter, an African American

mother who decided in 1965 to send her

seven children to all white segregated schools

by way of the Freedom of Choice Plan. As a

result, the Carters suffered house bombings,

intimidation, threats, even an eviction from

their home. Although I'm insurmountably

moved by the tremendous strength and

patience of Mae Bertha Carter, my heart

pumps eternal love for the fierce courage of

Constance Curry. In 1965, it would have been

taboo for a white woman such as Curry to

have any dealings with an all-black family

such as the Carters. Still and yet, while

suffering from the enhanced chance of her

death, she humbled herself and served others. What moved her to do so? Why did she feel so compelled to help? How can we take wisdom from the tireless effort that she put forward?

Many things come to my mind when I hear these amazing life changing stories. I recall a bible story I would like to shine some light on. At the beginning of the book of Joshua, we witness a variety of happenings. Moses is now dead, and the people have to accept another leader, Joshua. The book clearly states that the circumcised adults who left Egypt died in the process of wandering in the wilderness but what many fail to realize is that those who passed on were the fathers and mothers to the ones who were now inheriting the promised land. I'm quite sure there were times when many of them would cry themselves to sleep, reminiscing on the times they spent with their fathers and mothers in the wilderness. I wanna believe when special days like the Passover arrived, they would sit and think of the past Passovers when mom and dad were there. But the fascinating part of it all is that most of them mustered up enough strength to serve and fight while living under a multitude of suffering and pain. Things like this is what makes a dream or promise so significant because a great deal of pain goes into making it all come true. I once heard that a book written with no pain tends to be read with no pleasure.

Serendipity

When I first quoted the word serendipity, my mom said, "Baby, what does that mean?" I laughed to myself and gently replied, "It means to stumble upon great happenings by chance!" Serendipity means to look for one thing but find another thing that tremendously exceeds the prestige of the one you primarily sought after.

In 2014, I was a young, bright, compassionate youth minister who lacked wisdom. My life as a Christian was temporarily shattered overnight. I was deeply hurt by brothers and sisters in the church who made it their aim to capitalize on a public mistake I had made. These individuals never called my phone to pray for me, help me, nor serve me. They simply did what Pharisees do, find fault. I can almost remember the exact feeling. It overcomes me every time I recall the experience. I went through a series of emotions. Some moments I wanted to retaliate, but deep down I knew that would not accomplish anything. In fact, it would only make things worse. Have you ever been so broken that an individual could not pay you enough money to show your face in public? The thing about falling as a believer of Christ is that there will be those who surround you who cannot get past your failure. But the reality is that the blood of Christ has already lifted the burden of guilt and shame. However, there are people who will re-live your mistakes every chance they get.

Weeks after the situation, I remember telling myself how done I was with religion, religious persons, and could you guess what else? Yep, the church! I had come to a full conclusion that God was real. I loved him and therefore I could worship him alone at home. From the outside looking in, you would have thought I had lost my cotton picking mind, but really, I was content as the birds and the bees. One Sunday, I was on my way to Scottsboro, Tennessee. I was traveling there to fulfill a youth engagement that I had committed to months earlier. *"Extraordinary"* cannot describe the way God displayed his Spirit in that apartment-size church.

At the back of my mind, I was missing the pulpit but I had promised myself that I would never return there again. While traveling back to my then home, Florence, Alabama, I received a phone call from an old deacon of the West Gaines Church of Christ. He was an energetic being, full of laughter and wisdom. His name was James Bumpus. He had received my cell number from either Phillip

Goad or Jim Colins, two brothers in Christ that I cherish greatly. Brother Bumpus wanted to know if I would be interested in preaching one Sunday morning because they had just lost their minister to an unexpected relocation. He went on to mention that they had their eyes on three ministers to fill the position. I wished them blessings on choosing one of those ministers and I agreed to step in just that ONE Sunday. I had no idea what traveling to Lawrenceburg, TN would do to my life as a minister, a man, and a father.

My sermon title was called "Just One More Thing!" It was one of my favorites and I trusted in God that it would get those 7 or 8 members on fire for God again. He paid me, I left and headed home expecting never to hear from that funny old man again. In the meantime, I still was not attending a local church nor was I interested. My views on what Christ wanted for His church started to pull closer to His views and not what tradition had taught us. Tradition was the very reason why I was sitting at home on Sundays, instead of a sanctuary. All my life, I saw people leave the church because of people who attempt to take God's place through judging. Galatians 6 clearly tells the believer to help the wounded believer who is already broken, downtrodden, and who has repented.

Well, while in deep meditation one day, my phone rang and it was that old funny man again. He had got so comfortable that he called my Steve; no one calls me that but close friends and family. However, he spoke as if he had known me for years, so I laughed and smiled along with him because the guy was actually funny. He said Steve, the church has concluded on our new minister and "It Is You!" "Wait wait wait, I never told you I wanted to be your minister!" I told him I could not take it and that my only aim was to help them out that ONE Sunday. He replied, "Would you please pray about it?" I said yes and I ended up serving there for 3 years. Since then, the church has tripled in size. So there you have it., Serendipity. The word simply means to stumble on something great by providential chance. Now that I look back, the Holy Ghost had his hands on the entire chain of events leading up to this moment. My heart is now at peace with those who hurt me, and I truly thank God for their instrumental role in my purpose. There is an old saying to sum up this experience, "No pain-No gain."

Clarity and Conformation

When the angel spoke to Mary concerning her

baby, Christ the messiah, the holy one of Israel, she was moved with awe in hearing that God would grant her so much grace. However, months later, after speaking with her cousin Elisabeth concerning her vision, John the Baptist leaped in his mother's womb just at the sound of Jesus' name. This moment may have scared both of the women tremendously, but it most definitely gave Mary exactly what she needed for the service and that was confirmation and clarity. In the process of serving, we too need clarity and confirmation. This allows the server to have peace and serenity knowing that they are in the right position, at the right time. If, in fact one misses God's voice on where and how to serve, his grace will still somehow lead you to their appointed position. Yes, it may take longer, but through prayer and study, you will arrive. After reading a great deal on the life and work of Dr. Martin Luther King, I was tackled by the thought of God's providence touched on his life. He never wanted to lead a movement and he questioned God several times on his call to be a preacher. In fact, he had applied for a variety of jobs before taking on the lead pastor role at Dexter Ave Baptist church in Montgomery AL. The LORD's eternal power somehow closed all doors in the life of Dr. King, only leaving the doors of Dexter Baptist Ave Baptist church open, but why? The answer is easy, that was his divine purpose and position of service. He would have not made the same impact had he became a college professor or schoolteacher. All persons who are willing to serve God must know and realize that he has a strategic position for you and that he will never give you someone else's role. But I must say this while we are on this subject. Once the call upon your life becomes a great task, his grace immediately sends help that furthermore gives the believer confirmation. While Moses, being a fugitive and shepherd was tending the sheep, God spoke to him from a burning bush. After receiving heavy instructions, Moses himself was overwhelmed and was left feeling incapable of the task at hand.

Therefore? God in his gracious love sent Aaron to help Moses serve. So, there you got it. God does not take your position away, he simply sends the manpower you need to help you withstand and deal with the pressure that awaits you. And if the help never comes, you may have to go back to the drawing board to seek where you went wrong. So, after all, by God sending Aaron, Moses received clarity and confirmation which allowed him to have peace in his position as a moral leader.

Serving the forgotten

In this world, you will find all types of people. They will fall under diverse categories like the popular, the broken, the lost, the found, the

weak, the strong, the wealthy, the poor, the

remembered, and the forgotten. This chapter

will be centered around discussing the last

category of people, the forgotten. I'm quite

fond of this group because until recent, I did

not know they existed. You will never see

them on center stage waving at the big crowd

of smiling faces. They do not care to wear the

most fancy clothes and shoes. This person

normally keeps quiet, and remains reserved,

because for years, they have been taught and

trained to do so. Over the years, I was

blessed by God to witness a large majority of

these beautiful souls and yes, I did say

beautiful. While overseeing a detention center

of 43 juveniles and for the sake of confidentiality, I will not say the name, but I experienced something that will never leave my memory. As a habit, I would always make it to work 30 minutes early. While walking the unit one morning, little Bobby laid in his bed, wrapped under his colorful cartoon sheets, refusing to go to breakfast. However, co-workers knew that if anyone could get him to move with his group, it was myself. I do not know exactly how to explain it but God has always given me a way with understanding the pain of his forgotten people. While sitting on the edge of his bed, with one hand on his shoulder, I gently touched him saying," Son, Mr. Gill really needs you to go to breakfast and eat with your group. "I do not wanna go, I do not wanna go, I want to go home he replied while crying!" I really cannot say what it was but that statement pierced my soul like a knife through butter. After saying that, he simply said, "I want my mama!" Instantly, I began to think about my beautiful kids who were tucked away safely on that cold winter morning, and my lovely mother who was in South Carolina. And each of them would readily attempt to come to my rescue had I truly needed them. But the case of little Bobby was totally different. Going home for him consisted of much more than making a phone call. Family for him was DHR and the court system because his biological parents had proven that drugs and alcohol were more important

than loving him. So slowly and slowly he

drifted away on the ship of lost souls, only to

disappear under the rough waves of the

forgotten Sea. So Here I was looking into the

beautiful brown eyes of this child who for once

and again had no true ties to the outside

world. My heart must have jumped out of my

body and hid under his bed, just so it did not

have to constantly witness the pain I felt for

this forgotten child of God. So, whenever I

mention the forgotten, these are the persons

I'm referring to. They are in your churches,

schools, jobs, and within your family. They

have been broken, beaten, and abused.

These individuals live in silence so please do

not let the opportunity of serving them pass you by!

Listening to the forgotten

It is impossible to serve the forgotten if we do not have the patience to listen to the forgotten. Let us remember that they have already been cast down, trampled on, and destroyed. The last thing these individuals need is someone who will shut a death ear to their dying plea. This vital skill is very important and it is key to serving. An elderly sister in Christ once told me that we have two ears and one mouth for a reason. Jesus said it best, "he who has ears, let him hear!!!!!" Evidently, Christ knew the importance of listening. I can recall a time back when I myself realized how listening could truly save someone's life. For the sake of confidentiality, I will not mention his real name but for now, we will just call him Jim. This man played and has played a major part in my life. I remember when we first met. It was just an average day in the small city of Renova Mississippi. My friends and I were walking through Jim's backyard because it was a short cut to Mrs. Kelly's house. She was the candy lady. Well Jim walked out of his house and offered us a few dollars each for walking through his yard. In my mind I'm wondering why in the world would this old man pay a few dusty kids for walking through his yard. It would have made more sense to me if he paid us not to walk in his yard. From that day forth, a relationship began that is still eternally powerful to this very day. I would be at his door at 6am to learn a variety of things. He would take out the time to teach me how to fix cars, wash trucks, and build houses. One step at a time, he would instruct me on what to do and what not to do when setting up measurements, changing oil, and placing finishing polish on the chrome of his semi-trucks. I'm forever grateful for the things I have learned at the feet of that old generous man. It would be almost twenty years later before I truly understood his reasons for paying us to walk through his yard and giving us little odd jobs to do. He would later tell me that he did it because he did not want us selling drugs or stealing cars so he provided an honest way of gaining income. Well 20 years later, Jim called me crying. His wife was leaving him after thirty years of marriage. At this time, I was now Pastoring my own congregation. Jim listen for hours while I gave him spiritual insight on things that were going on in his life. Since that day he has called me every week when things seem to be coming against him. It is amazing how God places us in a position to listen to the broken, never knowing that the broken will one day listen to us.

"Motivating others!"

Life certainly has its share of pain, storms and brokenness. And many of us experience it on all levels. In fact, I think it is safe to say that sometimes the pain sticks around our front door like a stray cat that grandma continued to feed. And there are times when we crawl into the hole of life and just cry ourselves to sleep. This is what I call invisible pain and suffering. In the New Testament, Peter constantly warns us that like situations are bound to take residence in our lives. Since my ancestors dealt with similar pain and suffering, my question was, "How did they make it through?"

  The answer came to me like a shooting star

on a calm summer night. And the answer was

motivation. They were simply motivated by

those around them. During the harsh days of

African American slavery, Blacks were victims

of some of the worse treatments inflicted upon

human beings. They were tied up and beaten

with whips. Their women and girls were

sometimes raped and impregnated

unwillingly. Un-submissive men were burned

at the stake and lynched on trees for the

entire community to see. These things took

place on a weekly basis and the law

sometimes promoted and turned a blind eye

to this type of behavior. The days were long,

hot, broad, and hopeless. Over the dusty

cotton bowls, voices of negro spiritual would

ring out, giving the lost slave a glorious ray of hope. Most of these songs were written with a heavenly hope, causing the negro to believe again. However, freedom did not arise overnight. Soon the black man would discover one of the most powerful forms of motivation and that was religion. After the Civil War many slave owners were placed in a Strenuous situation where they had to let many of their slaves go free. Some overseers would allow these freed people to remain on their land to work as sharecroppers. According to Wikipedia, Sharecropping is a form of agriculture in which a landowner allows a tenant to use the land in return for a share of the crops produced on their portion of land.

During this time, both the free slaves and tenant slaves had the opportunity to gather at what they called the church house. Before they had this blessed opportunity, they would kneel by the window of the slave master's church and listen to scriptures being quoted and fiery sermons being preached. Much information was acquired but now they had the providential opportunity to practice religion according to what they knew and who they generically and historically were. Their services were both electrifying and spirit filled. In fact, many believe this to be their greatest moment after leaving the majestic shores of their homeland, Africa. It did more than provide hope to the negro; it equipped them with a sense of somebodyness, as Dr. Martin Luther King would to later go on to describe. Whenever anything went wrong, these Spirit led folks would make their way to the church house to call upon their God. These religious gathering could sometimes go on for hours at a time, depending on the purpose and what the spirit led them to do. Hearing powerful stories such as these still motivates me in time of doubt and worry. This same spirituality and power would later reform the world during the hateful days of Jim Crow through the movement.

Years ago, I recall working as a Unit Director at a Juvenile facility. Words cannot describe how much I learned while being there. Each day was a completely different experience and there were always amazing stories to hear from these kids. We had this one kid who was sentenced to complete the program. He was 17 and he made it very clear from day one that no one could not tell him anything and at the drop of a dime, he was ready to fight. At night, he would cry himself to sleep. At other times, he would cut himself with anything sharp and hope and pray that these self-inflicted wounds would lead to his demise. Like always, I would study and monitor the most troubled kids within the program, target the opportunity areas, and make them my personal mentees. While attempting to leave work one day, I discovered this young man climbing to the top of his closet and screaming threatening words to staff. One staff member asked me, "Mr. Gill, could you please try to calm him down?" Reluctantly I said yes!! While walking slowly in his room, I calmly sat down on the concrete slab of his bed. Looking up to him, I watched him act out for several minutes without saying a single word. He was expecting me to curse him, grab him, and use my power to my advantage but I did the total opposite. I allowed him to be the stronger and more aggressive one. After he got tired, I began to tell him how powerful he was. How I admire the books he had been reading. I even mentioned how great his poetry was. He excitedly replied and said,

"How do you know I write poetry Mr. Gill?"

Son, I sit outside your door at night and I listen

to you recite some of the most beautiful poetry

ever. His entire demeanor began to change.

His fist loosened to the point where his hands

were now open and relaxed. He then sat next

to me and told me his entire life story. The

report I built with him that day would be the

start of a wonderful mentorship. Many people

may read this with a heavy heart thinking I did

something quite miraculous, but that is not the

case. I simply MOTIVATED him! I Served

him!!!!

Made in the USA
Columbia, SC
08 December 2024